Let's Stay Together

Dating Made Simple

by

Dr. Marco Walder

We O.W.N Incorporated

P.O. Box 540861

Grand Prairie, TX 75054

www.marcowalder.com

Printed in the United States of America

Acknowledgments

I have been truly blessed to encounter hundreds of people this who have provided insight that has allowed me to create unique guide. First and foremost, I would like to give the honor and glory to my Lord and Savior Jesus Christ because without him, none of this would have been possible.

To Michael and Pat Walder who raised a ten pound twelve-ounce baby, thanks for all the support and love over the years. Without you guys, I would not be where I am today. To my sister Tara, thanks big sis for listening, giving feedback, and just doing what big sisters do which is take care of their baby brother. To my brother Rodney, thanks for being a great big brother; memories of walking to the bakery are priceless! To Lisa, thanks for your help and listening ears.

To my nephew Jeramie, watching you mature into a promising young man has truly been an honor. I would like to thank my entire family for everything that you have done over the past thirty-two years of my life. I love each and every one of you. To my cousin Billy Davis, "we are flying high like birds in the sky." A special thanks to my grandmother Ivory Waites; without her encouraging words while growing up, I would have never made it; may you rest in peace.

I want to thank Arabrian Lewis for her support. I also would like to thank Dr. Julia Ballenger and Asheya Warren for their assistance with this project.

To Earl Thompson, Charles White, Ruthie Bowens, Cassandra Gipson, and Darlene Morris, we may be divided, but we still stand together… I love you guys and thanks for the support; at first it was just a dream.

To all my friends who have endured the long discussions, I would like to say I appreciate it. Because so many of you guys have had a direct effect on this book, I would run out of paper trying to name each and every one of you, but to Brian Johnson, Jabari Johnson, Derodrick Ingram,

Sylvester Lilly, Jerrence Garrity, Daryl Jones and a host of others who helped as I created my thoughts for this piece of work, thanks from the bottom of my heart.

I also must thank two individuals who have been critical to my progression through life--- Carlton Smith and James Hicks. I cannot say enough about how I appreciate having you guys as brothers. To Carlton, thanks for keeping me motivated and pushing me to be better every day. Thanks for just being a true brother over all the years. To James, I would not be in the position that I am today without your knowledge and guidance. You truly are an inspiration and the sky is the limit. We are 90/10 "The Movement".

Last, but definitely not least, I would like to thank all the women who shaped my life's experiences with relationships; thanks for putting up with me and giving me the best you had to give. You will not be forgotten.

Dedication

I would like to dedicate this relationship guide to all the love souls around the world who desire that life-long mate....

Contents

Introduction

In modern times, we have witnessed a drastic change when it comes to dating. Women have become more successful, independent, and self-sufficient. This has altered some traditional norms that played a huge role in the dating process. Men, whom for decades were seen as the bread winners and sole providers for the household, have witnessed that role of being "The Man" diminished to being "The Compliment". For some, this change has drastically gone against what traditional opinions and perceptions have led us to believe a "Life Long" partnership should be.

I do not proclaim to be an expert on dating or relationships. I am just a man living in this time and era and my opinions, ideas, and thoughts are based on everyday observations and experiences. In my opinion you do not have to be married, in a relationship, or divorced to create a guide that may help solve a problem that many are having when it comes to dating in today's society. Yes, those experiences and particular situations could be very useful, but they are not always needed if the individual lives that life daily.

Make no mistake; the religious and spiritual perspective should be the driving force and ultimate instructional manual for finding a mate and maintaining a successful relationship.

This book in no way shape or form is intended to take its place. Instead, the words on the following pages should serve as a "generic blueprint" in modern society's quest of finding a mate to have a "true lifelong partnership" with.

Chapter One

Needs vs. Wants

Do you really know what you want?

In today's society, most of the problems or issues that many are facing with attracting a "lifelong" mate stems from deciding if the opposite individual is a Need or a Want. We define a needs something that you must have, it is a requirement, and it is NOT optional. A want is more or less a desire, something you crave, however, if not received, you can still maintain a sense of fulfillment because you have the minimum that you need.

I feel the only things that men and women need to survive is water, food, shelter, air and for those of us who believe in a higher power, a connection to that vital source. Keep in mind, a need is something that is required and is NOT optional. Let us take a deeper look. A person needs shelter to live. For example, an individual could want a $250,000 home, even though they may be unable to afford it. Until they are able to afford the home that they want, they should continue to be content and be mindful of their current budget. Their finances may dictate that they purchase a home. Although a cheaper home may not afford all the luxury and high end finishes they want, it will fulfill their basic need for shelter. Conversely, they can plan, strategize, and sacrifice to save enough money to be able to provide a substantial down payment that will lower the mortgage payment of the $250,000 home. By doing this, the family can likely stay within their budget range and also have the home that they want. Let us go back. The inexpensive home fulfills their basic need, which is shelter. Though it may not be as extravagant as the $250,000 home, it does serve the same basic purpose: fulfilling the need for shelter. In this example, settling for the "need" in the present is actually a positive step toward purchasing what you really "want" in the future.

In relationships, the habit of choosing our needs as opposed to our wants develops and cultivates the ultimate mindset for destruction. An individual should never look for a mate based solely on what they need. Instead, they should begin to examine themselves and look for someone that possesses the attributes that are wanted to make a relationship grow into a long-term committed union. When you look for a mate because of your unfulfilled needs, you're communicating that you are looking for someone to complete you. This could wrongly lead a person to speculate that you may not be ready for a lifetime partnership. If a void needs to be filled internally within an individual, they must first address those issues within themselves so that the lifelong mate they are seeking is not there to "complete" them, but instead, provide additional value to their already full life.

Individuals must first be complete themselves before they can serve as a complement to one another. The term complement is defined as something that completes, makes up a whole, or brings to perfection. Once a person is complete individually, then they have the potential to be a complement to someone else. The goal would be for both equal complements to join in a complete marriage.

A complete individual fully understands themselves and the facets that define who they are. These components include being prepared mentally, physically, emotionally, spiritually, and financially. Understanding all five facets is essential to truly being prepared to complement another person's life.

We all know that the "perfect" mate does not exist. Yet the perfect mate for YOU lives and breathes daily. While dating, an individual should never need another individual in the relationship. Understanding this key term is important because if you lose that individual or once they have met your need you tend to lose the urge to genuinely want that person, until you have another need that has to be fulfilled.

Oftentimes this is why most, if not all, men and women have or have had what is called a "friend with benefits". This individual's primary responsibility was to take care of that particular need you had at that time.

The need could range from paying a monthly bill to providing intimate pleasures. Once that need has been satisfied their level of importance declines. Think about it this way; a plumber's level of importance declines if everything in the house is operating and functioning properly. However, when a pipe bursts, the plumber's level of importance increases drastically because he is now needed.

We as individuals should want one another because ultimately, you will do more and appreciate more of the simple things this individual has to offer to your life. To want someone is really special because it is something about that individual that makes you truly want to be with them, which means it is optional, unique, and a choice. When you want to be with someone you do not mind sharing what you have worked hard for.

Most men and women between the ages of 20-35 tend to say they are "traditional" when it comes to dating. This is totally acceptable, but we must remember we are not living in traditional times so those standards and expectations that were possibly passed on by grandparents, parents, and other family members may need to be adjusted for today's generation of dating. I did not say change your morals and values, but be open-minded to making adjustments when it comes to dating.

Traditionally, the man paid all the bills, opened every door, and controlled ALL the household decision making, due largely in part to him being the sole income source in the home. Times have changed and that is no longer the case in most modern households. Women are just as successful as men in today's society. Most women are very independent and self-sufficient, so they do not need a man to do many of the things that his grandfather or father did when they were dating.

Most women simply desire a great "complement" to complete them. If a person between the ages of 25-35 tells me they are a "traditional dater", I tend to say that is not true. You may simply have some traditional views and standards that you support and agree with. I also try to inform them that in today's society, dating relationships have evolved from traditional standards and it is impossible to date in the same manner that previous generations did. In the past, people were only able to converse on the phone or go to that person's home with parental supervision or permission. Today's technological advances allow constant communication through text, email, Skype, and social networking, resulting in expanded dating communication scenes.

The logistical dynamics of dating have also changed. Instead of picking a young lady up at her house for the first date, most women now prefer to meet you at the desired location.

With these constant shifts in the dating game, people MUST also adapt or risk feeling lost and left out.

As I searched within myself, I realized I desired a mate whose main characteristic was sharing. I desire a mate who is willing to share in all facets of a relationship. These ways include physically, mentally, emotionally, spiritually, and financially. I feel if two people are sharing in all facets of a relationship, no one will feel as if they are pulling the load. Most people seek another mate or source of relief when they are in a relationship and their partner is not pulling their load or forcing the other person to do more than normal on a consistent basis. So my focus is making sure that my mate is willing to share all the responsibilities that come with having a life-long partner.

When I meet an attractive young lady (because we are visual creatures), during casual conversation I ask the simple question, "If we were to go out on five dates, how many would you OFFER to pay for?" Now this question may not work for you, yet it works for me being that I want a lady that is willing to share. Let me reemphasize, I only asked "how many would she OFFER to pay for", which is different than asking how many would she actually PAY for.

You may suggest that this is not a good measuring tool to determine whether she is a good woman or not.

Again, this question addresses my desire of wanting someone who does not mind sharing, so your question could vary. I selected this question because a lady can go out on seven dates, seven days a week with seven different guys and never spend any money IF she chose not to. For a man, this is rare and requires much more work because that is not how the dating arena was constructed. Also, if we go out on five dates, which could be within a three-to-six-month period, there has to be a mutual interest of some sort, right? If there is not a mutual interest, you probably would not make it past the first date. So, if she is willing to sacrifice something she has worked hard for just to get to know me, I feel she is truly interested.

Because sharing is extremely important to me and is my number one WANT, the lady's response to the question allows me to decide if I would like to continue getting to know her. If her answer is zero, I am respectfully moving on because this indicates a potential sign of selfishness or an overly traditional standard that she's likely not going to change. As we all know, you must be unselfish in order to have and sustain a healthy lifelong partnership. If a lady responds, "Well, it depends on how much I'm into him or how well I know him," I will still move on because it should not matter how well you know him if you are truly willing to share in the dating experience.

Let us look at another example: if a man said that he would take you out to dinner only if he was allowed to come back to your place afterwards, how many women would still consider going on that date? I would venture to say not too many. Now, if she says that she would offer to pay for any number of dates other than zero, with no stipulations or hesitations, then I continue to get to know her because my main want is someone who does not mind sharing. Genuine answers do not require deep thought because they are rooted in truth and are natural responses. Again, this is the question that I created based on the most important want that I desire: sharing.

While searching within yourself to find your particular want, you must use a simple process that will allow you to focus on the right characteristics you desire your mate to possess. Your core question should be, "What is the most important characteristic they must have?" Then you must ask yourself if you can deal with the "catch 22" that accompanies this characteristic. For instance, I often hear people express that they want their future mate to be honest. This is a great core characteristic, yet the "catch 22" is that they can be too honest and if they know you want the truth and nothing but the truth, that is what you are going to get-- the truth. For example, you have gained a few pounds and you try on a dress that you still have from a few years ago.

If you ask for his opinion, you must be able to accept him saying to you that you may need to lose a few pounds or that the dress is too tight, without taking it personal and penalizing him later during the week when he attempts to be intimate with you. Guys, you may say you want a woman who is hard-working. If so, you must accept her working those long hours to meet that deadline at work on a day you planned to go out to dinner. In addition, not seek to penalize her later in some sort of way because she is committed to working hard.

Now let me forecast what my particular question actually allows me to conclude. If she is willing to share in the beginning, then she will most likely continue to share until the end. If she does not mind helping now, if we got married she probably would not mind sharing or helping with the bills and other duties in the household.

Relationships that develop into partnerships require that you start off the way you want to finish. Most people find change uncomfortable, so why would you attempt to create something within someone that was not there in the beginning? You may say, "Well she can say and tell you what you want to hear". I would say, "You are right", but remember you can always put a person in a situation to see if what they say is actually true. I also believe that once a person tells you how their actions would look, this gives you a measuring tool in which to observe them.

This allows you to see if their actions match their words, which can build trust and respect if they prove to be aligned with one another.

My typical first date is a meeting at a coffee shop. This is a great start to really get to know someone because it forces both individuals to communicate and it is inexpensive. This is a great first meeting place because if you do not like what you see or hear it is a minimal loss. On the other hand, if you do, this was a great gain with a minimal loss which is a win - win situation. The second date may be a nice yogurt or ice cream parlor. Again this forces communication and it is inexpensive, so the loss factor is minimal and the gain can be enormous. Most men make the mistake of starting out how they do not plan to finish. An extravagant first date is a setup for disaster if your lifestyle or way of living cannot consistently provide that. Stay true to who you and your budget are, and always do what you know you can maintain for a lifetime. By doing this, it will save you from a lot of disappointments and debt.

One could say, "You are just cheap and scared to be burned." I would say to them that they are totally right!

Who wants to be burned? I have never known a broke cheap person, have you? Now going to coffee shops and ice cream parlors does not mean you are cheap, it just means you have a plan and a purpose. This can also show that you have an appreciation for the simple things in life. If I must take you to an expensive, upscale restaurant in the beginning to impress you, then I do not want or need you. Remember, there is someone for everyone. Do not settle for what you think you need, rather go after what you know you want.

Let us move forward. We are two dates in and by this time I should know if I would like to continue pursuing this person based on the conversation and some other topics that I will cover later in other chapters. If so, I would now probably arrange a meeting for a happy hour or an early lunch to continue the process. This scene will allow us to communicate and get to know one another, but in a more traditional setting. Notice I said, "happy hour or an early lunch."

This keeps the potential loss to a minimum and if for some reason it does not work out, the gains are still in your favor. Avoid the movie date if at all possible on the first couple of meetings. This is truly a risk because it does not allow you to really get to know the person.

Additionally, after a movie usually comes dinner, so the man may end up with an expensive tab and no gain. By the third or fourth date, the lady has usually offered to pick up the ticket, and being the gentleman that I am, I would not allow her to pay anyway. It is the fact she offered that we as men care about. So this was a win-win situation and she was true to what she said.

That is always a good situation when a person stands by their word.

Ladies, this also works in your favor because this allows you to offer to pay for a date that will be inexpensive and a very minimal loss for you as well. However, if he allows you to pay for any date other than the first one do not look at him differently and please do not offer if you truly do not want to pay.

Sometimes men will go out of their way to do things that they know they cannot keep up to impress you. So be open and honest up front. Stay within your comfort zone and do not be afraid to "put him in a situation" that will show if he's a man of his word. If you prefer phone conversations vs. text messages, express that in the beginning. Also, be flexible because he may be growing in the communication aspect and may need some time to adjust to your preferences. Remember, change is uncomfortable for most people and it happens over time. Women can get the world from a man by only giving up a city if you look at them as being part of a checker board vs. a chess board. We will cover more on that topic in Chapter 4, "Three Things a Man Wants".

Knowing what you want is crucial when searching for a mate. People should desire a relationship in which you do not mind taking one another out on a date or just doing for the other individual just because.

Feeling as if you need to do something for someone has a lot of drawbacks. So try to do things for the other individual because you want too. This eliminates that feeling of needing something in return after you have done something that you truly wanted to do. A man desires a kiss goodnight after he has taken you to dinner to satisfy his need to know if you like him or not. However, if he does not need that confirmation he will most likely end the night with a soft handshake or a respectful hug. At the end of the next date, he will likely get what he wanted at the end without even asking for it; this is checkers not chess.

In the process of deciding whether you truly want an individual, make sure you are focusing on the right wants and being realistic. For instance, do you choose to hang out with her because she makes you laugh or do you want to hang out with her because you feel she may allow you to become physically intimate with her? Do you really have a connection with him mentally and he is really great company or you do not have much in common, but you do not feel like cooking and know he may treat you to a meal if you ask him to meet at a restaurant? We must truly differentiate our needs and wants in order to accurately know what we desire in a life-long mate. Remember to desire the right wants to be effective and true to the other individual.

Activities

LST Task 1

Create a question that you can ask when you first meet someone. This question will be proposed during the initial conversation. Their answer will allow you to decide whether you should continue to pursue an individual based on the most important want you desire from your life long mate.

Example: Desired Want – Sharing

Question: If we went out on five dates how many would you offer to pay for??

Chapter Two

Standards and Deal Breakers
And the list goes on and on…

"He does not meet all the "standards" on my list." "She has kids! That's a "deal breaker" for me." As I composed this chapter, I reflected on how those terms are tossed around by both males and females so frequently. In doing so, the terms "standards" and "deal breakers" have become totally misconstrued.

After a long day at work, I went to a local restaurant for a cocktail. While seated at the bar, I sparked a conversation with an attractive young lady. After breaking the ice and asking the routine questions (name, status, career, education, etc.) I internally classified her as having what I call "potential" to be a lifelong mate. Remember that phrase because I will explain exactly what that means later in this chapter. The conversation was very nice so, we agreed to exchange numbers. I politely told her that it was a pleasure meeting her and to have a nice night as I exited the venue.

The following morning, I sent her a text stating that I enjoyed her company from the previous night and that I looked forward to speaking with her again.

I hurried home after a hard day of work and settled in for this great conversation that I was so anxious to have with this "potential" lifelong mate. As I dialed her number, I began to gather my thoughts and strategize my approach to engage in a stimulating conversation. She answered the phone and our conversation continued from where it left off the night before. The small talk was good, however now it was time to learn more about who she really was and what she desired. I asked her what was she looking for in a mate and what were her "deal breakers". She instantly went into calling off a list of things: "I'm really wanting a friend; he has to be over six feet tall, he must believe in God, must have a Master's Degree, clean cut, has to love family life", and so on and so on. As she continued talking, I began to think that this young lady did not have a true grasp on what she should desire in a life-long mate. This particular individual didn't have a clear understanding of what "deal breakers" and "standards" were and how they differ.

The same can be said for men. Men dream of this video vixen and the idea of having a lifelong partnership with her without focusing on whether she meets our deal breakers versus how beautiful she looks. Men also tend to pick out a "trophy". This type of lady is one who has nothing more to offer other than her outer beauty which can be misleading when it comes to choosing a potential lifelong mate.

Men often desire the "trophy" because this may determine the level of how society and their peers view them.

This young lady wanted a friend, which can be taken the wrong way by an individual looking for a lifelong mate. That phrase could lead the other person to believe that she is not interested in a committed relationship, which may not be true. Of course, we all want our lifelong mate to be our best friend, but why waste time searching for a friend when you truly desire a husband or a wife. If the individual makes it to the ultimate goal of becoming your husband or wife, it's likely that at some point and time within the relationship they will become your best friend and much more. Let us reflect. When you plan to take a trip to a certain destination, you rarely worry about the stops in between because the main purpose is making it to the final destination. So if you tell a person you're looking for a friend, nine times out of ten, all you will find is a friend. If you're truly looking for a life-long mate, I advise you to effectively communicate that desire in the beginning and take the appropriate steps to find your mate.

One of the most important components in the process of finding a life-long partner is deciding what your individual deal breakers are. Deal breakers are those things that cannot be compromised no matter what. For example, in my opinion, religion would be considered a deal breaker.

For most, this is an important connection that we desire in a life-long mate, which means we will remain constant with our views and beliefs. A standard, which many view as a deal breaker, is very different. Standards, unlike deal breakers, can be compromised if some other aspect or characteristic trumps it. Wanting a partner who is six feet tall is a standard because it can change if the individual meets your deal breakers or some other feature that draws higher interest, which means it's adjustable and open for change. When you create your deal breakers, be precise; have a quick list. Devote more effort on finding someone who meets your deal breakers versus your standards. These qualities will lay the foundation for the partnership.

We all have heard that a house can be repaired as long as the foundation is sound. Therefore, spend more time making sure the foundation is being laid one perfectly placed brick at a time. Avoid the long list of demands because the longer the list the fewer prospects you have. Also, be specific and realistic when you create and ponder on these factors. Don't have "Real Housewives" taste and you are only qualified for "Good Times." Don't pretend to be a "Bentley" when you are really a "Kia". There is nothing wrong with thinking highly of yourself, but don't forget to be realistic and true to who you really are.

Before you become offended by the previous statements, take a minute to analyze what these statements mean.

Make sure you are qualified for the same thing that you seek in a mate. Be able to show that you are able to meet or go beyond those expectations without becoming someone you truly are not. Many times we desire something that we ourselves cannot attain, but feel we need in order to be happy. For example, if you only possess a high school diploma you should not discard someone who has a GED. Yes, they are different in the realm of education, but that does not truly tell whether the individual is less likely to be successful or a good mate. If you make $150,000 a year, try not to overlook the lady who makes $50,000 a year. She may be a great mother who understands a true partnership. I did not say, "lower your standards", however be realistic when you are searching for who and what you want. Bring those things to the table that you are willing to share unconditionally that makes a person WANT you. Reduce the prerequisites a person must have before you give them a chance.

The term I like to use to describe deal breakers is non-negotiable. I tend to use both words to give a clear understanding of exactly what I am asking. This leaves no room for confusion or miscommunication, which many partnerships tend to face from time to time.

These are qualities that one must have and can never be compromised, no matter what, because they set the foundation.

First and foremost, they must believe and love God. For many, religion is at the forefront when it comes to deciding on a mate. In my opinion, I think two individuals who view religion differently will eventually develop spiritual separation. This can be compounded if kids are involved because the question arises of who do they go to worship with or do they even participate in organized worship?

Secondly, she has to be a non-smoker. This deal breaker speaks specifically for me because I truly do not have the desire to date an individual who smokes cigarettes. Some may say this could very well be a standard and you are totally right. This could be a standard for you, but for me this is a deal breaker because I am just as passionate about smoking as I am about religion.

Finally, she must be able to perform two of the three C's: COOK, CLEAN, and/or be able to CARE for a family. Notice that I required two of the three; I am equipped to perform all three so which ever quality she lacks, I am able to carry the load because remember, this is a partnership. This is also aligned with my number one want -- SHARING. When considering your deal breakers, aim for three, but no more than five.

The object is to have as many prospects as possible so you are better able to find what you want. It is nothing like taking a knife to a gun fight --- you have no chance of winning; and our object is to win.

To conclude this chapter, remember: the objective is to identify, define, understand, and classify deal breakers versus standards. Desiring a man who makes a lot of money should not be categorized as a deal breaker. Sure, we all would love to be financially well off, but if he loses all his money what do you have left? Desiring a woman who has a body like a goddess is definitely not a deal breaker because we will someday grow old and if that is your foundation, your house will fall. Men and women frequently say that a lack of physical stimulation from the other gender is a deal breaker. Well allow me to inform you that if this mindset supersedes all the others on your list when it comes to deal breakers you will have a sex-ship instead of a love-ship. As you prepare to set sail, I am sure we all know which ship will sink first. If you ever question whether a quality is a deal breaker compare it to one of your other potential deal breakers to gauge its importance. I often hear people talk of the 80/20 rule. This rule simply means that your main companion only provides 80% of what you need in a relationship which gives you reason to seek another individual to provide the other 20% which will make you 100% complete.

I am a firm believer that if you build your 80% by first knowing what you want and secondly seeking someone who meets your deal breakers it will keep you faithful when that 20% comes knocking at your door because you will remember and appreciate how rare and special your 80% is.

When I developed my deal breakers, I compared every standard to religion because that was at the top of my list. Allow the deal breakers to be an important part of the foundation for any partnership because standards can be changed. If you lay a strong foundation and build off the principles of your deal breakers, everything else can be worked on. Do not forget you are supposed to grow with one another during this process of becoming life-long partners.

Activities

LST Task 2

Create three to five deal breakers and list them in order from one to five with one being the most important.

Deal Breaker Examples:

1. Religion

2. Non-Smoker,

3. 2 of the 3 C's

Chapter Three

Three Things a Woman Wants
Boarding the ship to Venus

We have looked deep inside ourselves and revealed various answers to questions that we were unclear about as it pertains to what we want from our mate. We have also gained an understanding of the key components and meanings of "deal breakers" and "standards". A solid foundation has been laid to build our search process for our lifelong mate. Let us board the ship to Venus and take a deeper look into the three things a woman wants.

Men often express that they have difficulty understanding women. They feel that they have done everything they can within their relationships to make her happy and this effort is still not good enough. Many men become emotionally, mentally, and physically detached. These facets can lead one to stay committed to a relationship that is unsatisfying and unhealthy. If this is or has been you, listen up: it is not what you are doing that destroys a relationship; it is the LACK OF what they WANT you to do that causes the confusion. Oftentimes, men tend to look for reasons to become the victim instead of searching for ways to become victorious.

For example, no matter how hard you exercise, if your diet (which is the most important component) is unhealthy, you will not lose weight. The same principle can be applied when it comes to a woman: no matter how hard you try, if the effort is not focused in the right areas of what she wants, she will always feel empty and you will feel over exerted, causing tension between the two.

Women only want three things from a man. You may ask, "Why only three?" Remember, the more things you focus on, the less you are able to maximize your effort. This turns your gain into a loss and our mission is to WIN with minimal loss.

Women are seeking three things from men: SECURITY, STABILITY, and AFFECTION. They desire a few other characteristics, but ultimately if you master these particular wants, you will satisfy a woman and keep her happy for a lifetime. Let us examine these three wants to gain a better understanding of what they actually mean.

Security is defined as the degree of protection against danger, damage, loss, and criminal activity. Women want a sense of security from their mate because it allows them to reach their comfort level with you. Most women who grew up with their fathers involved in their lives are often "daddy's girls". They simply feel safe and protected when they are in daddy's arms. They feel as if he cures all things and can conquer anything.

This is what a woman desires when they are with their man. This assures them that if anything happens he will stand up and protect them as their daddy would. Now, for those ladies who were not raised with the care of their father, this type of security may take some time for them to adjust to. They are probably pretty independent and strong-willed because they were forced to be.

In no way does this mean that a woman who grew up with their father in their lives is weak; they just have more access to a constant security blanket in the male form. How many of you wonder why most women want a man who is over six feet tall or at least taller than they are? The reason is because his stature provides a sense of security. A guy who is taller allows these particular women to reach their comfort level. This is really desired for women who are tall or like to wear tall heels. Gentlemen, do not panic if you are less than six feet tall because if you recall in Chapter 2, this should be a standard. A woman will observe how you comfort her in the midst of danger. They will look to see if you are committed to putting their safety before your own. This is crucial if you desire a woman to trust you as her protector.

Once security has been observed and provided, they look for stability. This word stems from the root word stable. We will use the adjective form to better understand its meaning. Stable means to be firmly established, fixed, not changing, or steadfast. Women want this because a man's stability can project or even predict how their future could possibly be. Now men, we have all been in an entertainment complex or at a venue and an athlete or someone who is famous enters the room. Most of the women may desire to see, meet, or cordially greet this particular individual. For some, they become "groupies" and desire a financial or personal gain from these individuals. It is not because he is better looking than you, but rather for the most part, he is financially stable, which means he can provide a lifestyle for her that she may not be able to provide for herself.

Do not be upset or think she is not worth your time; that is just human nature. Every man would look at Beyoncé or Serena Williams differently if they were not financially wealthy. I am willing to wager that 99% percent of the men who are not as financially wealthy as Oprah Winfrey would marry her right now regardless of Chapter One and Two because she could provide them with a life that they may not be able to provide for themselves. It is human nature to desire a level that is higher than yours. Women want a man who is stable. Simply put, have a career and a plan that includes dreams and goals not only for you, but for your future partner and family. Have a vision and allow your vision to be seen by her through your day to day actions. Develop a work ethic and be determined to foster success in all that you do. This also means be reliable, dependable, consistent, and more than anything else, take care of your business.

Also, this means being able to provide for the household and not take away from growing as a family and as partners. Last, but definitely not least, a woman wants affection.

Affection is a rare state of mind or body that is often associated with a feeling or type of love. Basically, this means understanding and managing a woman's emotions. Most men struggle with this because they have a problem with their "pride". This can often stand in the way between effectively communicating and understanding what your mate is going through or trying to convey to you. Affection can be as easy as motivating her to do something she struggles with or as demanding as turning off that exciting football game to allow her to vent about something you may feel is not that serious.

Affection is the true essence of a woman and men must occasionally allow her to verbally express her emotions. While allowing her to voice her concerns, stay firm and give her good advice, but be actively engaged in the conversation. Most people will take advice if they have been given the opportunity to release everything that they had built up inside. When they are not allowed to release everything stored inside, they tend to shun any type of constructive criticism.

After the wall has been put up, you tend to hear phrases like, "you never listen to me" or "you think you have all the answers" or "it is a waste of time talking to you, you just don't understand". Once this trend has been developed, this could lead to the cause of your 80% seeking a 20% because the 20% listens, which could lead to a snowball effect of events that can really destroy the partnership.

A true example that many of us have witnessed comes from when we talk about physical pleasures provided by the other gender. In no way shape, or form does this self-help manual promote pre-marital sex, however, we will touch on a few topics that pertain to intimacy in a relationship. Typically, the task for the man is to stimulate the woman so that she climaxes (if he really cares about her physical wants). The majority of women do not climax during every intimate encounter, but 99% of every man who is able to sustain an erection throughout intercourse will climax. Now as a man, if you remove yourself from her presence after you have climaxed and go to the restroom or go into the other room to do something else other than cuddle with her; you are going to have a hard time enticing her to become physically intimate with you at a later time.

The reason for this is very easy: where is her reward, what does she get from allowing you to entertain and embrace her temple physically.

Remember this is not a fling; this is your lifelong partner. Again, I reiterate in no way shape or form am I advocating pre-marital sex, but we must address the key role intimacy plays in relationships.

The object for both individuals is to win and at this game, a woman wants to win just as bad as you do. It is harder for some women to climax than others. Instead of leaving, stay beside her; cuddle have a light conversation. Caress her and show that you are affectionate and that you really care about her wants just as much as you care about yours. If you are able to do this, your level of affection with your lifelong partner will blossom. Strive to be a good listener and not one who only listens with a negative ear. Devote more energy on trying to understand her view versus trying to be understood. The object of communication and dialogue in a relationship is to connect with one another but many times we allow our emotions, pride, and selfishness to make that attainable principle an illusion.

The key to understanding a woman is being able to unlock the three wants and understand how each component works with your particular mate. The level of each want will be different depending on your particular mate. Be able to adjust accordingly and know exactly what your mate wants and focus your efforts in that direction.

Remember, women were created differently for a reason and it is the man's duty to learn how to grow with her in order to sustain a healthy lifelong relationship. We were ordained the leaders and the head of the household so it is up to you the man to plan, prepare, and provide those essential wants that will allow her to trust you and follow you unconditionally.

Activities

LST Task 3

List the three things a woman wants and under each component identify a characteristic that you possess that will allow you to be able to support each want.

Want #1 – Security

Characteristic you offer that meets that want: Example: I believe in protecting my family above all.

Want #2 – Stability

Characteristic you offer that meets that want: Example: I attended a trade school and have been in my career field for over 10 years.

Want #3 – Affection

Characteristic you offer that meets that want: Example: I am a great listener and communicator.

Chapter Four

Three Things a Man Wants
Boarding the ship to Mars

As we board the spaceship of relationships, our next stop will be the planet of understanding the Man. This creature has been a common factor in relationships since the beginning of time. The Man is considered the source of all human productions. The Man has a greater challenge when it comes to understanding what he really wants because the advancement of the woman has altered his position tremendously. So, as we circle around Mars, we will make a few stops that should allow a woman to truly understand the wants of today's man.

The Man is a different creature when it comes to satisfying his wants. Notice I did not say when it comes to satisfying his needs because we have established that the objective of this book is to focus on wants rather than needs. We will still stay true to the principles that were set forth in the previous chapter when we discussed the wants a woman desires.

A Man only has three major wants when it comes to his woman.

If a woman is able to focus and master these wants, she can successfully understand today's man. To no surprise, an important want is sex. I know you are reading this and saying to yourself that the entire universe knows that, however I never take it for granted that everyone knows and understands that. Men also want loyalty, which is a vital component in today's relationships. Finally, a man wants respect for his manhood. These are the key wants a man desires in a relationship. We know there may be a few more, yet these are the ones that will stand out and enable a man to take the next step and move towards marriage.

As stated, we are not promoting premarital sex, but we are analyzing how intimacy impacts a relationship. Sex is the first component we will discuss. It stems back to the days of Adam and Eve. Sex or Sexual intercourse, is commonly defined as the insertion of a male's genital into the female's genital for the purposes of sexual pleasure or reproduction. Now for the alternative meaning -- sex means satisfying every extreme! Yes, you read correctly; satisfying every Extreme!!! Men go to exotic dance clubs, watch pornography, read adult magazines, and physically lust for women that they picture in fantasies. For a man, this is natural because we are visual creatures.

While in a committed relationship, if a couple has agreed to become physically intimate and the woman decides not to physically appease her man for reasons she has chosen, she could be possibly making one of the biggest mistakes in their relationship. If she decides to abstain from having physical intercourse for spiritual or religious reasons this is something that both parties will need to take time and discuss. This is a genetic want that we as men must have -- it is human nature. The decision to abstain is one that both individuals must agree with in order to maintain a faithful and healthy relationship.

I have spoken with numerous individuals who say that they have not been intimate with their mate or spouse in months. I think to myself that their relationship is headed towards disaster. The worst thing a woman can do is take away something that men were built to do, especially if she has already provided him with that satisfaction. Physical intercourse does not simply satisfy a man, it can boost his confidence, self-esteem, and overall appreciation for his woman because of the physical and mental connection. Just some food for thought -- this act of connecting can work in the same way for the woman, which is a win-win situation for both parties. Studies have shown that couples who are intimate on a regular basis have fewer problems than those who are not.

The straight message is this: if you are not intimate with your man, do not be upset if he goes or does something else to satisfy that want. If you are in a relationship that has already vetoed that law, make sure you keep up the process until both parties agree to abstain from this activity! Remember, BOTH parties must agree and if not you may have to part ways with one another.

Ladies this next statement will provide valuable insight when you start the process of choosing your next mate. A man who desires a wife does not have SEX at the top of his list when it pertains to choosing his lifelong partner. When the male gender matures they tend to view life and love differently and strive to seek a true partner not based on their lustful ways, but on the potential she has to be a loving and faithful wife. This brings us to the number one want that a man who desires a wife seeks: loyalty.

A man who desires to be a husband has matured and understands that he is meant to have a wife. He will search for those unique qualities in a woman that show she is capable and ready to be his supporter. This quality is displayed through acts of love and unselfishness that will not only suggest, but confirm that she understands how to be loyal. The reason a dog is known as man's best friend is because dogs have demonstrated loyalty to their owners and this truly represents the key component a man who desires a wife seeks.

The want of loyalty will carry the most weight when it comes to deciding if the woman is his potential lifelong partner. Loyalty is defined as faithfulness or a devotion to a person, country, group, or cause. The best example that comes to mind is from the movie Hustle and Flow. The movie is about a man who had three ladies that he once used for different purposes. One lady was an exotic dancer, another lady provided intimate pleasures for money, and the last lady took care of the kids, house, bills, and every other issue that needed the attention of the household. His job was to keep the money flowing into the house daily. Of the three ladies, which one would you assume he cherished the most? If you said the one who took care of the kids, house, bills, and every other issue that needed attention, you are totally correct. She was his support system, the rock he could lean on. She stood beside him and kept the house together no matter what and he knew she would never leave him. As a woman, when you reach this level in your relationship, your man recognizes you as his backbone and he knows that without you, he is nothing. With this mindset, he will do anything to keep you, and yes, I do mean anything.

To a man, a woman who is not loyal is truly less of a potential wife in his eyes. It is funny how men view this trait.

He can go out and cheat on his woman and expect her to take him back as if he is entitled to make a mistake or stumble during this walk in his relationship. Yet, if the woman commits the same mistake, he is ready to walk away, no questions asked. I was unable to understand that thought process until I looked at it from the view of ownership. To a man, his woman is his property and no man wants anyone messing with his property. He will protect his property by any means necessary. After I took this concept and viewed it from this perspective, I understood why men are ready to erupt when it has been discovered that a woman has been unfaithful. Being loyal is something that one cannot imitate. This characteristic starts from within and must be a part of a woman's make up. If you desire a husband, spend time developing trust, faithfulness, and reliability. There is nothing greater than knowing you have someone there for you unconditionally and that will support you not only in the midst of the highs, but will stand even taller in the midst of the lows.

The final want of a man is respect for his manhood. Manhood can also be described as "pride". Pride is an inward directed (feeling) emotion that exemplifies either an inflated sense of one's personal status or the specific, mostly-positive emotion that is a product of praise or independent self-reflection. This particular emotion has poisoned millions of people worldwide.

This want has landed many individuals in places that we as a society strive daily to avoid at all cost.

A man's pride or his manhood is a want that many hold to a high standard because he knows that if he does not have the respect of his counterparts he may become a victim of a disease that may plague him for the rest of his life. When a man feels as though he has lost the respect of someone he loves it can be devastating. This can be emotionally, mentally, and physically damaging which could lead to a man acting out in ways those we as men and women will not support or condone.

Nonetheless, for a man, this is what cannot be destroyed by anyone, let alone his mate. As men, we must maintain the feeling that our mate respects and views us as a man. Many times in relationships, a man may fall short in efforts to be the best man he can be, but when his woman voices this and acknowledges his doubt, this can be very dangerous to the relationship, especially if this is done amongst friends or family members.

When a male feels this trait is no longer respected, he may choose to take extreme measures in order to regain his self-respect or his pride, which can and may lead to physical abuse. If you notice I said a male "feels", for this is not an action a "man" who is secure with his manhood will choose to take.

As his woman, try to uplift your man even if he falls short on some things. Avoid lonely friends and those who have experienced horrible relationships because they can instill negativity and provoke you to act in a way that is unhealthy for your relationship. I've seen various groups of women out enjoying a nice meal and I look at their body language to get a feel for the tone of their conversation. Many times I see one lady whose body language speaks of being disgruntled and irritated- she is the one you may potentially avoid when it comes to discussions about your significant other. Yes, she may be a good friend, but she could be a horrible communicator which could ignite something between you and your mate that may not have escalated if you had not spoken with her about the situation. It is great to have a positive friend who is honest, yet understands the true essence of communication to talk to about situations. Remember, be careful about what you share when it pertains to your mate, for it could come back to haunt you.

Many factors can contribute to a male questioning his manhood. One may struggle with low self-esteem, being physically abused as a child, or he may not understand how to control and deal with situations that pierce his pride. Those who can manage their pride have a great handle on standing for the right things in their life. Men are sensitive creatures with an outer extremity that many feel must be impenetrable.

Yet the ones who learn how to become one with their emotions will allow their pride to add to them instead of ruin them.

In conclusion, men are simple creatures who can be all that you want them to be if you understand their makeup. Take time to observe your man and examine the areas that maybe detrimental to his growth as a man. Be his lover, his biggest fan, and most importantly, become his support system: a rock he can lean on and he will love you to no end.

Activities

LST Task 4

List the three things a man wants and under each component identify a characteristic that you possess that will allow you to be able to support each want.

Want #1 – Sex

Characteristic you offer that meets that want:

Example: High Sex Drive

Want #2 – Loyalty

Characteristic you offer that meets that want:

Example: I would show loyalty by making sure he has lunch for work daily.

Want #3 – Manhood

Characteristic you offer that meets that want:

Example: I would not challenge his manhood by disrespecting him in front of family and friends.

Chapter Five

Do Opposites Really Attract
The Laws of Physics say they do, but do they?

For years that old saying, "opposites attract" has plagued millions of relationships and people struggle to understand why. Who really desires to spend a minute, let alone a lifetime, with someone who is totally their opposite? Take a step back and look at a few examples. A person who loves sports will more than likely be attracted to another person who loves sports. The lady who loves to cook will probably be attracted to another person who also loves to cook. A guy who loves to workout will have a better chance making a connection with a woman who enjoys working out. It is really simple, yet we choose to complicate this untrue saying because we have not prioritized what we love versus what we like. The object is to find someone who likes or loves to do what you love to do because it makes you more willing to compromise on the things they love to do that you merely like to do.

The laws of physics state that a positive charge needs a negative charge to be sustained. While this is true for physics, this concept produces a negative charge when it comes to relationships. When analyzing your potential mate's hobbies and interests, you should seek to have at least 70% of the same similarities in common. The reason you should not look for the entire 100% is because we still need room to grow with our mate and be open to new adventures. You should seek to have various interests in common which will foster regular, mutual enjoyment. The purpose of companionship is to enjoy life with another human being.

We tend to meet people who are totally opposite of who we are and wonder why later down the line we could never connect. The answer is a simple; it was doomed from the start. There were few similarities to keep one another on the same page and connected in the beginning. This leaves room for separation and options which is always a set up for trouble because this person has never moved into position to become a priority. Be realistic and understand that you will not find someone who enjoys everything that you like to do. Take some to time prioritize those things that you love to do in comparison to those things you like to do. A person may love to watch football, but only likes to go to live games. So which one should take precedence? Finding someone who really likes to watch football, whether it is at a sports bar or at home should be your focus.

It is also a plus because every once in a while, as a couple you may be able attend a live game.

Attending a live game would be considered optional because the priority is being able to watch the football game together. Pretty simple, huh? I thought you would agree. It is simple because we have moved from playing chess to playing checkers. Many times we overlook the simple things which turn into big problems later down the road when we are in a committed relationship. My goal is to train and prepare you to pay attention to specific details that can assist you with developing a keen eye that will allow you to focus on those key details that play a huge role in your daily life.

It does not benefit you to focus on the entire puzzle if you do not understand the importance of every piece. Finding an individual who enjoys many of the hobbies and interests you do may seem difficult in the beginning. However, this method can prove to be very effective as your relationship grows over time. Connecting with an individual who has similar interests can be very simple and satisfying if you implement the proper principles and strategies that can be tailored specifically to fit you. While writing this chapter, memories of the song, "Just the Two of Us" by Bill Withers came to mind. His lyrics really summed up this entire piece in a nut shell… It should be just the two of us, just you and I.

Our mission and goal is to win, so the easier we make it, the better chance we have to master our plan and work our plan of finding our life-long partner.

Activities

LST Task 5

EXAMPLE: Life Activities

Love to Do's

1. Staying at home and watching sports on TV

2. Staying at home and watching a DVD

3. Eating out at a restaurant

Like to Do's

1. Going to live sporting events

2. Going to the theater to watch a movie

3. Staying at home and cooking

Chapter Six

No Investment, No Return

If you just plant seeds, the crop simply won't grow… It needs water

A man walks into a bank and tells the bank teller he would like to withdraw funds from his checking account. The teller asks the gentleman for his account number and he provides it to the teller. As the bank teller began to look up the gentleman's account. A peculiar look came over the bank teller's face. The gentleman immediately asked, "What is the problem sir". The bank teller cautiously tells the gentleman, "Sir, you currently do not have any funds in your account and it shows a balance of zero." The gentleman calmly asked, "How could that be possible? I do have a checking account correct?" The bank teller replies, "Yes, but your recent activity shows that you have not made a deposit of any kind to this account, so you do not have any funds to withdraw. I am sorry sir, but we cannot help you, have a great day." The gentleman slowly walks away without displaying any emotion of any kind.

You may be wondering, why did the gentle man go to the bank asking for funds from an account with a zero balance.

Well, he assumed by opening a checking account with a bank, he would receive a return without depositing anything into the account, which we all know is not true. In relationships, people tend to grow dissatisfied with the level of commitment and the effort the other person is providing in comparison to their own. This could have been a sign displayed early in the dating phase that was overlooked. When this happens, it leaves room for the feeling of emptiness, which leads to this particular individual becoming selfish and less giving because they assume the other individual has elected to do the same. While dating and in a relationship, no one wants to feel as if they are always doing all the work or pulling the majority of the load. We all would like to have someone who does not mind assisting and is willing to help every now and again.

Consider the sport of weightlifting: a weightlifter who desires maximum gain wants a spotter for those last few repetitions that alone he would be unable to perform alone. The same can be said for two people who join together with the intention of having gains individually and as a union. They both must be willing to be one another's spotter during the entire journey. For the weightlifter a spotter does not appear in the middle of a set, or when the lifter begins to struggle and needs their help.

The spotter is present at the beginning of the set with their full attention given to the weightlifter to make sure they support the weightlifter in the best way possible. Sometimes the spotter provides support when they feel the weight is becoming too heavy for the lifter without the lifter giving any type of physical or verbal notification that they are in need. It is the spotter's duty to be able to sense when assistance is needed, even if it is minimal. The weight lifter will welcome the spotter's help tremendously because it helps him or her continue to pursue maximum gains.

In a relationship, the object is to be your mate's spotter. This element is crucial to the longevity and appreciation that each mate will have for one another during the course of a relationship. For many years, people have assumed that their role of being the spotter should take place only after the relationship status has been defined with clarity; that is, boyfriend, girlfriend, or dating exclusively. Looking back at the traditional standards when it comes to dating, this particular mindset was a norm. However, we are planning and preparing to be successful in today's era. Unfortunately, this type of thought process is a method that has destroyed many relationships of today. Take a deeper look at this assumption and focus on one want from each mate.

Let us start with the man. Remember they want loyalty? Sure you do. It is one of the three wants a man has to have. The best way to show a man that you can be loyal is by being his spotter. This trait is not displayed after he asks you to join him in a committed relationship, but rather this trait should be visible at the beginning, during the dating phase, and should continue throughout the relationship. In today's era many use the word dating incorrectly which I believe has created many of the problems we deal with when it comes to investing in a potential life-long partner. Dating is defined as a form of courtship consisting of social activities done by two persons with the aim of each assessing the others suitability as a partner in an intimate relationship or as a spouse. If you are seeing multiple people you are merely entertaining prospects, not dating. Make sure you select only one individual at a time to date.

Another key component is to relinquish all ties to the other options in order to maximize your efforts when it pertains to displaying those qualities to the one you elected to be priority.

The want of loyalty could be shown by picking up a tab, picking up some clothes from the cleaners, or simply offering to take him to lunch sometime. If you can implement this trait into your dating phase it will pay dividends later on in the committed relationship phase.

For all the guys beating their chest right now, you might want to relax. We also learned that a woman wants security and stability. What better way to show her that you possess these qualities than by being her spotter? One of the hardest things for a man to do is mature to a point in his life where he can focus on one woman. It has been portrayed over the decades that a man with a plethora of women was regarded with high respect in society. This perspective is one of the quickest ways a man can lose a loyal woman. These actions will not reveal to her the want of security. Once a man has reached a level of maturity to understand what is required as he prepares to find his life- long partner he will be able to rid himself of immature temptations and desires. Demonstrating the wants of security and stability can be as simple as recognizing that her car is dirty and offering to wash it or have it detailed. Maybe you arrive at her house and you notice her yard needs to be mowed. Offer to have it cut or find the time within your schedule to trim it yourself.

Many times we say what we will do once we are in a committed relationship, but we all know that actions speak louder than words. Also, be selective with the terms and promises you make because those expressions provide a measuring tool that your actions must add up too.

People buy into what they can see. I always say, "Sell a dream to someone which is asleep because they are the only ones who will buy it." Dating is about taking risks in order to receive a reward. If you never step outside your box and take a chance, never question why you only receive minimal rewards. A weightlifter who does not take a risk with heavier weight will only achieve minimal gain. However, if he adds a spotter, he has a greater chance of achieving maximum gains. Invest as much in the beginning as you would want to receive in the end. By asserting this type of effort if it does not work, at least you know that you gave it your all.

Activities

LST Task 6

Go back and take a look at your number one want and list a way your mate could be your spotter.

Example: (1) Want – Sharing

Answer: Paying the Utilities

Chapter Seven

So Fresh and So Clean

Step out new and improved, with a new attitude

The experiences that one will encounter while dating or in a committed relationship often create an adverse feeling that can reduce the desire for a life-time mate. This particular feeling usually arises after a failed attempt to find love in a previous relationship. The term used to describe this type of feeling is called baggage. Baggage can be defined as the physical, emotional, mental, and sometimes financial experiences or behaviors from our past that we allow to alter our steps in the present. Baggage often dictates the direction of our steps on as we continue to seek a life-long partner.

The past is called the past for a reason. It is used to indicate something that is gone by, elapsed in time, or has formerly been. In short, it means it's over, done, and can never come back. If it does, it will never be like it was before. Many times, people allow their past relationships to define how they handle present and future situations.

The downfall to this is that if their past relationships and experiences were very traumatic and emotionally stressful, the baggage can become a villain while on their search towards happiness. Others use their baggage to become better equipped for their next journey. Either way, everyone has baggage and we must be able to decide what baggage to keep and what baggage to discard.

In this chapter we will analyze all the ways that negative baggage can destroy future joys. Notice that I said "negative baggage," because all baggage is not bad. Some past relationships provide insight into one's self which motivates and allows the individual to take strides towards becoming a better, well-rounded individual. For our intents and purposes, we will concentrate on the "negative baggage" that can remain with a person for a month or as long as a lifetime. This is what many conceive as a person being overly guarded, difficult, or just not ready to pursue or be in a relationship.

Negative baggage can be created from many different sources. The individual may have been the person's first love or someone they gave their all too in every facet of the word. Negative baggage can also stem from mental, physical, or financial abuse. A committed relationship can put an individual in financial peril requiring years of recovery.

It also could stain an individual with memories of being abused physically and verbally which can tarnish even the finest of jewels. Negative baggage can be created from anything or anywhere. This type of feeling can dwell within a person for a long period of time. The longer a person conceals this negative baggage, the more pain and heartache it will bring to them. It is often present in their daily conversations. Listening to a person who is packed with negative baggage can be harmful and depressing. So be careful when speaking with people who display this type of baggage and attempt to engage them in healthy conversations that can uplift one another.

Positive baggage are the experiences that we have learned from and have used to improve ourselves and become well-rounded individuals, not a bitter person. I often hear people mention growing and becoming better, yet they display actions of someone who is totally unapproachable or just a terror to be around. These types of people usually feel they are better than before when actually they have become worse. Regardless of when, where, or how, the negative baggage was acquired, it must be cleansed if this individual wishes to become better. This negative baggage must be replaced with positive baggage before a person can start a new healthy relationship.

You will never be able to mentally get rid of something that has made you the person you are today which prompted the chapter's title, "So Fresh and So Clean" for we will be renewed once we are done.

As an example, consider a new car. Over time, this once-sparkly, shiny, brand new car will go through different situations that will eventually make it the car it is and will be. Whether the car is sitting outside during a severe hail storm, being scratched at the grocery store by a cart that was blown by the wind, been involved in an accident, or been dented, chipped, and smashed, this car will change.

All in all, no matter how many times you have this car painted, repaired, or fixed, it will never be the way it was when you bought it--- BRAND NEW. So what do we do? Some pull out the dents and cover the dings with a fresh coat of paint. Many add new rims and tires or install a new radio. Most add tons of other bells and whistles that will make the car feel and look better than ever. The only way we are unable to remodel our car is if the car is totaled in an accident. Only then, will we be forced to start the process all over, by first deciding what we want. Unlike a car, the only way we can be totaled out is if we pass away. We must focus our efforts on being repaired, fixed, and repainted. By seeking the right guidance and information this will add new accessories to your life.

This will show the world that we are fresh and clean inside and out. For some, this may mean a new haircut or hairstyle. Others may want to lose a few inches and get in better shape. This may also mean digging deep within yourself and revisiting some of those dreams and wants that while in past committed relationships you were unable to fulfill. Whatever the case, this has to take place before you will be able to give 100% to the next potential life-long mate.

The rehab process can be a difficult one and takes time, so seek assistance from a respected source that can assist you in making a smooth transition. The hardest thing to do is get over something alone. There are many different resources to help you do this. How long would it have taken the Romans to build temples in Rome if one person had to build each temple? Probably a very long time; even more time than it originally took.

I often encounter people who say they are not ready for a relationship. My usual response to them is to ask, how will you know when you are ready? Will a bell that ring like on a microwave when food is cooked? Oh wait! You will just know!!! Please! You're fooling yourself. No matter how much you think you are ready, you still may not be ready and just when you do not think you are ready, may be the time that you find out that you really are.

Remember, minimal risks will reap minimal rewards; high risks allow the chance of yielding high rewards. Let us look at the religious perspective. Many tend to state the phrase, "I'm waiting for God to send me my mate". I wonder have they ever thought that God is waiting for them to fix something in their life that will allow them to truly love and embrace the one he has selected for them receive. Expecting a fruitful result without preparation and a supreme effort will only grow a continuous pathway to failure. As you wait for God, allow him to witness your work as you prepare to be a life-long partner. We will focus more on the religious and spiritual perspective in Chapter 12, "The Bottom Line".

Now, when you are rebuilding your house of baggage, make sure you keep your eyes and ears open so you can recognize and avoid strangers and those individuals whose sole purpose is to be a guest. These individuals will look and act like something you want, however deep down inside you know this is not what you desire as a lifelong partner. Many times we go through a phase of trial and error only to discover we are dealing with more errors. When you get back out there and start dating, remember to use what I have taught you and you will see that calculated risks will bring forth sought after rewards and deter those who aim to punish you.

Always remember, "If you are never scared or embarrassed or hurt, it means you never take any chances". - J. Sorel

Take a chance for Love!

Activities

LST Task 7

Think about the negative baggage that was created by a prior committed relationship and how it affected you or your next relationship. Give an example of the negative baggage and how you were able to turn it into positive baggage.

Example: (1) Ex-mate was not a big supporter of my recreational sports activities. This created a filling of emptiness inside of me because I valued having my mate attend those games from time to time for support.

Answer: Make sure whenever I meet someone they like sports or participating in recreational activities.

Chapter Eight

Everyone Plays the Fool

Fool me once, shame on you; fool me twice shame on me...

Ever question why he only calls you after 10 p.m.? Maybe you only receive a text message early in the morning during work hours saying the generic, "Have a Great Day". Have you ever thought about when the weekend comes around, she is nowhere to be found; yet Monday through Friday, she is always available to chat and mingle? Could you be the one who he only invites to come over and watch a movie instead of going out to a nice location to sit and talk? Still wondering why you can never pick her up from her place or why you always have to meet him out at a local restaurant or bar? Well maybe they are married, in a committed relationship, or have chosen to keep you as an option and not as a priority. Don't feel bad; everyone has played the fool at some point in a committed relationship or during the dating phase. This usually leaves us feeling ashamed, tests our pride, or has us questioning how we allowed ourselves to have the wool pulled over our eyes.

We pride ourselves in taking the time to evaluate an individual before we decide to commit to getting to know this person. Many of us ask people who may know these individual's questions that may provide insight about them. Some even go as far as doing a background check just to make sure these individuals do not have a criminal record, a bad credit score, or anything that would be considered a red flag that would force us to disengage from the possible connection. We often date people and later find out that they may have more kids than they originally said, they are not single, but "separated", they lied about the career field they worked in, and a host of other misguided statements also known as lies that we fall victim too. Do not take this personal, but no matter how much monitoring, background checking, snooping, spying, and all the other James Bond investigative strategies we employ, you still can end up playing the fool sometimes. As I stated in previous chapters dating, relationships, and love all require taking a risk. Many times those risks do not bring about rewards.

No matter what era of dating we are in, one thing will always remain constant: Trust is one of the most important components in a relationship and will always be one of the most vital elements in sustaining a committed union. If you do not have the ability to trust, your relationship will be a roller coaster ride from day one.

Once the trust in a relationship is gone, the relationship is definitely headed in the wrong direction. The longer these two individuals stay together, the more the little things will begin to slowly tear them part. A simple missed phone call or text message that ordinarily would not cause an argument now escalates to a full blown disaster, which could lead to a verbal or physical altercation. This type of behavior can also be considered as abuse and we do not condone that at any point on your journey to finding your life-long partner. Working those long hours with John to meet deadlines which was normal now becomes questioned accusations of having more than a "working" relationship. That weekly guy's night out now becomes an awkward situation by accident as she was "just in the area" and stopped in to say hi.

The definition of trust in its simplicity means reliance on another individual or entity. In a relationship, this means being:

- ☐ Honest

- ☐ Loyal

- ☐ Committed

- ☐ Responsible

- ☐ Dedicated

- ☐ Dependable

We will take the time to reinforce these words. Honesty refers to an aspect of moral character and denotes positive, virtuous attributes such as integrity, truthfulness, and straightforwardness along with the absence of lying, cheating, or theft. William Shakespeare may have said it best, "Honesty is the best policy." -- Remember the familiar word Loyal, which refers to the concept of loyalty which means faithfulness or a devotion to a person. Committed is a key word which many in today's era struggle to grasp an understanding for. It is a promise, an agreed attachment, usually in the sense of being associated with an individual personally. Responsible, another vital component means being able to fulfill one's obligations and able to be called upon to answer for one's acts or decisions. Dedicated, is one of the things those who really love one another understand is required in a relationship. This means to devote to a divine being or address as a compliment.

Did you happen to notice another key word we became familiar with in previous chapters? Finally, dependable this simply means capable of being depended on. In a committed relationship there will be numerous times where you and your mate will have to depend on one another to sustain your relationship. Please do not get this word confused with need because we have learned that need is a requirement you must have, yet if you are depending on a person and they cannot accomplish the task you can complete the task yourself because you are already equipped to do so.

These are just a few simple words that mean the world to many singles and couples. Trust is a word that the tongue can confess, but the body must submit to. Many of us tell our mates daily that we trust them, yet our actions demonstrate otherwise. One thing about trust is that no matter how much we try to speak it into existence, we must be able to see those adjectives in our mate in order to build our confidence and give us that security to avoid falling into the pitfall of assumption. When I meet a young lady or pursue a relationship, my trust meter starts at 100% because each new person deserves an honest chance. I only use my past experiences to keep me from walking down the same path of wreckage as before.

People have been betrayed by their past and they just assume the next person is seemly the same. This way of thinking is a major mistake. Many people fail to realize that their actions are what keeps a person close and their words are what runs them off. We must learn not to tag a person with a label or pass judgment on someone before they are allowed to demonstrate the truth of who they really are. One thing we all know is that over time, the truth will eventually be revealed. Remember, we have cleansed the negative baggage so the better person in us thrives to seek positive experiences and interactions so we start off positive hoping to end positive.

During the encounter, things that you want to pay attention to will start to become visible. This will happen not only visually, but verbally. For example, if you are on a date and the individual cannot be torn away from their cell phone, you may want to make a mental note of that. While on a date, both parties should be able to detach from their cell phones because the object is to focus your attention on getting to know one another. You may want to keep a close eye on the time arrangements of your dates because what they can do at night time should also be able to be done in the day time. If he is unavailable during the day or only reaches out at night, there may be cause for concern. I am not advising you to look into every action with the mindset that this could be a potential sign, but I am saying that when it comes to trust and a person being honest, we do not want to short change ourselves.

We want to make sure that we have done our homework and classwork before taking the test. The object is to put ourselves in the best position to be successful, or to simply win. So as you start to see subtle signs, make adjustments on your trust meter, however, make sure you can confirm the tendency before validating the action. In other words, do not make decisions off an assumption or a guess. If needed, pose the concern to the individual and allow them the opportunity to be truthful and honest.

This will allow them the chance to confirm your speculation or assure you that your trust is not being jeopardized. By them assuring you that your trust is not being jeopardized, you begin to form a bond, conversely if you find out later down the road that this bond was made on a faulty foundation, (pending the severity of the infraction), lower your trust meter appropriately.

Once your trust meter for that person falls below 70%, it is time to nip this potential mate in the bud and move on. Just like in school, anything under 70% is a failing grade and we all know that you cannot make it to the next grade unless you have passed all of the appropriate courses. Unfortunately, you may encounter a catch 22 similar to school where a teacher may grade on the curve. The one where you actually earned a 65% in the course, but your score was graciously rounded up to a 70%; even then over time, that once gracious gift will turn into a lifelong curse that will take twice as long to recover from. So if you know right, then you need to do right; if you do right, you put yourself in a great position to get the right results.

As I bring this chapter to a close, remember to treat every new encounter just as it is--- a new encounter and to give each individual an honest chance. Give each new individual the benefit of the doubt until their actions show them to be different. Allow your actions to represent your words and your thoughts. Continue to grow from past experiences and allow present advancements to guide you to develop a trust for someone who has the potential to be your lifelong mate. Stay focused on your course until they give you visible reasons not to. Over time, your trust will grow and this will be a key component as your relationship becomes stronger day by day.

Do not let your need to be with someone put you in a situation where you look at the truth with a false eye. This means seeing the obvious, yet forcing your mind to perceive a justifiable answer or outcome is in the near future. This is another key reason why we should focus on seeking the characteristics that we want in a mate. The feeling our human intuition attempts to provide us is usually validated by a person's actions. However, when we are faced with a situation that could pierce our heart, we tend to view reality as a picture of illusion. Although many are blessed with 20/20 vision, they too can be deceived. The false eye view has clouded all of our minds and hearts at one point or another. If you are already in a committed relationship, the struggle is to connect the dots. Believing half of what you see and none of what you hear can be a setup for disaster.

During both the dating phase and in committed relationships, it pays to listen to a majority of the things you hear. This allows you to verify those words against the actions your eyes will see. The visual perspective of a situation or a particular behavior can prove to be very valuable to the heart, mind, and soul. This perspective can also allow a person who is uncertain about an individual to confirm their words based on their actions. This is crucial when you begin to search and evaluate those who have the potential to be your lifelong partner. If we stand still and watch the world go by, it will.

Many times we meet people and choose to sit back and wait for their "true-character" to present itself. As you wait for them to run out of lies and false intentions, you may find yourself wasting valuable time entertaining Mr. or Mrs. Wrong. Allow your ears to guide your heart and your eyes to cement that individual in your soul. Listen to their words and connect those dots with their actions. Remember, if the dots do not connect you and that particular individual will not connect. Do not hesitate to inquire about certain words, actions, and behaviors you observe that may be damaging to a committed relationship. These strategies can help an individual avoid a "Truth" their ears and eyes wish their heart will not have to encounter.

Activities

LST Task 8

Think about a time you prejudged someone and later found out your assumption was totally incorrect.

Example 1: You assumed a lady was high maintenance because she always carried a designer handbag and wore designer clothes, yet she enjoyed the simple things like sitting at home watching a movie or cooking.

Example 2: You assumed a man did not desire a committed relationship because he was not going all out to win you over in the beginning. Instead, he was taking his time to get to know you by coordinating simple dates and outings.

Chapter Nine

In Love vs. Love
How deep are you willing to go...

Our journey now takes us to the "Land of Love" or for some "Heartbreak Hotel". This is the place where emotions run high and the pain can be found deep within the soul. This place is where two people can come together and unite for a lifetime or divide in a matter of seconds. It is where compromise and sacrifice walk hand and hand. This is the place where the fortitude and will of both men and women is tested. As we enter, be prepared to have a life changing moment because love is a gift for some, but a curse to many.

Love is an emotion of strong affection and personal attachment. Many people like to get deep and philosophical with the meaning and spruce up the interpretation, however on our board; we are playing checkers not chess, so we will continue to keep it simple. Do not be surprised if you do not see words like eros, agape, or platonic. Those words are very powerful and have a deep meaning when it comes to understanding love. However, my method focuses on simplicity not complexity.

I often ask people of all age ranges, ethnicities, and relationship backgrounds which they would prefer. Is it important for them to be in love with their mate or to love their mate? I posed those two questions to couples who had been married 15 years or more.

The answers I received varied tremendously! The majority of these couples wanted love. Additionally, I asked if after being married for a substantial amount of time were they still in love or did they love their mate? Again, the majority said they loved their mate. Now for me this was not a shock because I understand the difference between being in love and loving your mate. I also posed these questions to couples who had been together 10 years or less. The majority of these couples said they preferred to be in love; however, those answers came from many couples who were one-to-five years into their relationship or marriage. Those couples with five- to-nine years vested in a relationship or marriage gave mixed views. I turned to those who were single and desiring a mate and the majority of their responses fell into the being in love category. I will explain why the viewpoint of "loving" your mate is the one that we should desire to understand and live for.

Many assume they know the difference between being in love and loving your mate, but many have been drastically misguided.

Let us examine what it means to "be in love". Think about a time in your life or a romantic movie you have seen where best friends have met up at a local bar or restaurant for drinks and dinner and the, "how is your relationship going" question came up. There is that one member of the group in a relationship and he or she is really happy. You usually hear the following conversation: "So how is the relationship going?" "To tell the truth, it has been great! These three months have been the best of my life. I really think I'm in love." Then that unexpected pause in the conversation comes and the other person asks, "Do you really? What makes you think that?" Then the reply, "I would have never thought that I would meet someone who really understands me. To have someone who cares about life just as much as I do. To be able to have someone who shows me that they care and in turn treats me how I always wanted to be treated. They really complete me!" They continue with several other romantic phrases that bring the feeling that life could not possibly get any better. If only this feeling would last forever, but it does not.

Four months later, they are in a committed relationship, but things just are not the same as they were the first three months. The person, who was initially head over heels in love, is questioning themselves daily as to why and how they got in this situation. The answer is very simple; you focused on how someone made you feel.

You found happiness in what they were doing to you and what they were doing for you. To chase something that can run out is like driving down a dead-end street. Once you reach the end, there is nowhere else to go. This will leave you thinking and guessing what to do next.

Take for example two people who are newlyweds. They will experience what many refer to as the "honeymoon" phase. This phase usually last between six months to three years before reality sets in. What reality you ask? The one that leaves one or both parties realizing that they are married and wondering if the "relationship" is going to change now that this new "title" has been established. If you committed to getting married solely based on being in love, it will not last because again, being in love is not what you are doing for them; it is what they are doing to you. Being in love is also about how they made you feel. This feeling led you to believe this was the person you needed in your life. I used the word need because more often than not, the feeling that they are giving us was a need that we did not come to grips with while we were single.

I remember asking a lady why she married a gentleman I knew and she was at a loss for words. After a few minutes went by she said, "He treats me like a queen." Do not get me wrong; we all desire someone who treats us well.

However, what happens if that person stops treating us in the way that makes us "feel" good? Most people decide to end the relationship and seek another individual. Some remain in the relationship and it becomes filled with lies, deceit, and adultery. Being in love is a feeling that comes and goes.

It can be here today and gone tomorrow. For example, many couples renew their marriage vows. They often recreate this moment because somewhere during their relationship, that being in love feeling reappeared and it is greater than before. Before I move on, I will bring a better understanding to you about being in love. There is nothing wrong with being in love. I am a true advocate and believe it is a key component to a committed relationship. Make sure when you make decisions in regards to your committed relationship, they are not made only from the feeling of "being in love".

Let us take a look at what love is. We all know or knew of someone who was in a relationship and was contemplating leaving or staying. Maybe you know someone who is in a rocky relationship and it has hit a rough spot for any number of reasons. During conversation they may share how they have been with their significant other for almost 20 years and they do not know if their relationship will make it. They may have lost interest or elected to be unfaithful in their committed relationship.

They do not talk to their mate the way they used to and everything seems to irritate them. Nonetheless, with all the issues and problems they are facing, they remember the commitment they made. The commitment to stay with their partner through the good and the bad is the guiding principle they use to determine whether they stay or go. For some, this principle may not be a concept that they select to subscribe to. That is the difference between being in love and loving someone.

Now for those of you who love your partner, as opposed to being in love with your partner, you have reached the point that I refer to as "The Concrete Stage". At this stage you become stubborn, naive, blind, strong, understanding, set in your ways, two of a kind, and a ton of other things which would take an entire book to list. Most importantly, you have started on the path to becoming life-long mates.

I have watched couples who have been married 20 years or more go through routines when they are together. The couple usually starts to dress alike and almost even look alike. They don't bother one another too often and they are really simple when it comes to one another. They have a tendency to know what the other is thinking or is about to say. The couple has come to know their mate so well that they know how to push their buttons and when not to test the water.

When you reach the "Concrete Stage", the feeling of investment has over taken any notion of walking away. You would rather deal with someone you know before stepping out into the dating scene again and try to build something with someone new. You could even know that your partner is being unfaithful or dishonest about a situation yet, you value the time and effort that you both have put into one another and turn a blind eye to the problem. Your love for your partner and the partnership you have built will force you stay together just for the sake of the kids.

True love is when the relationship is not about you; it is about the other person or an entity that is bigger than both of you. Some couples stay together because if they got a divorce the financial division would be such a hassle it is not worth the time and effort to deal with.

I have seen couples who have been married for over 40 years still enjoy one another as if they were just recently married. We all have seen an elderly couple and when one of the individuals dies away, it is not long before the other is laid to rest. Love is something more powerful than anything we will ever see on the face of this earth.

Love will make you do things you never imagined doing. It can cause you to deplete your bank account for your loved one.

It can destroy your life if not carefully handled. Love can make you blind to obvious facts and issues that if you were not in love would be easily detected. Most people love unconditionally and once you have experienced that type of love and someone takes it away, you either want it again or you do not. That is the biggest reason why older people choose not to re-marry because once you have given your all, it is hard to go back and do it again; yet even they can be cleansed and trained to love again. To love is rare and for those who reach that point, it really takes more love to walk away from it. I remember loving a young lady so much that I had to walk away from her because we were doing more harm than good to one another. Yes, I wanted her, yet I knew we were not meant for one another; so instead of being the problem I became the solution. To this day, we both agree that was the best decision we ever could have made and we both are better because of it.

As we come to the final turn in the Land of Love I hope I was able to clear up the assumption that "being in love" is better than "loving" someone. Both serve their purpose, however when it comes to deciding if the individual is a lifelong partner; do not rely on what they can do for you or how they make you feel. Instead, focus on your primary want because this is the trait that will be your guide when you begin your journey to the "Concrete Stage" which is the ultimate of all stages LOVE.

Activities

LST Task 9

Create a question that you can ask when you first meet someone. This question will be proposed during the initial conversation. Their answer will allow you to decide whether you should continue to pursue an individual based on the most important want you desire from your life long mate.

a) Give an example of what being in love looks like.

Example: He made her day when he brought her lunch on his off day.

b) Give an example of what love looks like.

Example: She paid the light bill after he misused the bill money.

Chapter Ten

Hard Worker by Day and A Fantasy at Night

Make sure once you clock out you are ready to clock back in....

Guys, we all have that one female co-worker that we sometimes fantasize about. You know the one I am talking about. She enters the room, and every man instantly focuses his attention on her. Her hair, smile, scent, and beautiful eyes bring a smile to our face when she approaches. However, it is not just her physical attractiveness that intrigues us. It is also the way she carries herself: professional yet feminine. It is her work ethic and the quiet strength she exudes. She does her job and does it well. She can also can engage you in conversation and make you feel like you are the only guy in the room. She does not attempt to be a distraction, for she truly is about the business of her job and her career at all times. Nonetheless, when she walks past in her business suit heading towards the conference room to lead a meeting, she automatically dictates a "rise"; a response from even the smoothest gentleman.

Ladies, you have the same type of guy on your job. You may not want to admit it, but there is a gentleman that you all look at as the epitome of manhood.

He has the looks, education, career, and style that can put Idris Elba and Matthew McConaughey to shame when it comes to fashion. Every strand of hair on his head is flawlessly trimmed and edged as it connects with his perfectly groomed mustache. When he approaches, all direct their attention to him. Just like the guys, it is not just his physical presence, but also the way he excels in his profession. When he leads a meeting, he provides you with a tantalizing experience that alters your seated positions and forces you to concentrate on what is being talked about and not what fantasies his mere presence is bringing about.

There is nothing more enticing than an individual who can step out into the corporate world and compete with the world's best.

A person who on a day-to-day basis can present a stature that everyone in the office desires to have. Unfortunately, they cannot because these individuals are happily married or in a committed relationship that means the world to them. Others in the office wonder how these individuals can come to work shining as vivid as sunlight daily. They ponder how these two people are able to operate as if life could not possibly get better. Well it may have something to do with them knowing that once the work day is over, a night full of passion and pleasure awaits them when the work night starts.

If you need to go back and read the title of this chapter please do, but I will help you out. If you desire a strong relationship that keeps the spice in both individual's life, give as much energy at night to your relationship as you do during the day to your job. In other words, continue to be a hard worker at work, but make sure you give the same amount of attention to being that fantasy in the bedroom at night. If you are able to balance this transition, you will keep home at home and give no reason for your 80% to seek that 20%. It lets your mate know that all those fantasies they may have can be fulfilled right at home. This provides both mates with the assurance that they not only have someone who will work hard in corporate America, but they will work just as hard to satisfy them at home, which in this book is a win-win situation.

Many times in committed relationships and marriages, couples allow the thrill to disappear to. God designed men and women to enjoy intimate encounters in a committed relationship (namely marriage). If we were not built to enjoy this experience, it would not feel as great as it does. There is nothing like knowing there is no limit with your mate when it comes to leaving no stone unturned behind closed doors. This can add flavor to a committed relationship that one or both partners feel things have become mundane. If you can provide maximum effort to your mate behind closed doors, you add much more than just great intimacy to your committed relationship.

We all know that couples who are intimate have less stress than those who are not. It also gives them a great opportunity to connect and bond. The force that can be generated within the confines of four walls, four doors, or even four halls can be life changing. Therefore, if we know that this particular act can provide so much reward, why not indulge in it to the utmost.

I remember growing up and when some of the guys would talk about lustful encounters, we all would frown at some of the things we heard people engaged in doing. For example, it was a true no-no to perform oral stimulation growing up. Now it is very common and some people even enjoy giving oral stimulation more than being orally stimulated. Many ladies felt it was totally disrespectful to have intimate encounters in a car. Now that is one of the most thrilling places to pump out thrusts and moans while shifting gears in a mustang. The older we get, our outlook on a lot of things definitely change, so why not continue to have a different outlook when it comes to satisfying your mate. No one wants their intimate encounters to become routine because just like every other routine, it gets boring really quick. Then we search for another "routine".

Do not allow the work day to consume your work night energy. This means you have to take care of yourself, workout, eat right, and learn ways to rejuvenate your body.

For some, this may mean a relaxing bubble bath complimented by a glass of wine. A nice massage for your mate after a long day may just be the trick that turns on their light switch. If you feel like you are running short on ideas and things to do, get on the internet or visit an adult store. Be open to growth when it pertains to intimacy the same way you are in the work environment. Strive to be better daily. If you take this attitude with you when you and your mate are alone enjoying the fruits of your labor, when it is time to pleasure one another, it will be as easy as a walk in the park.

Activities

LST Task 10

List three ways that can ease the stress of a long day at work that you would like to do with your mate.

Examples:

1.   Dancing

2.   Massage

3.   Walk in the park

Chapter Eleven

Living Life or Just Living
While the getting gets good, the good has to get better

The motto for most singles is to live life to the fullest. So why does this motto change when singles merge into a committed relationship? Some may say that once you have kids, things change or they may mention how career demands require more travel or that the long hours are very difficult to work around. Many say they do not have as much freedom as they did when they were single, but should you? Others blame it on the fact that the characteristics of their mate have slowed them down. For example, their partner is no longer as outgoing as they were when they first began dating. Whatever excuses, and yes I said excuses, you use make sure that you shoulder all the blame because it is truly your own fault.

The purpose of a committed relationship is to find someone who you can share your life with, and based on our prior chapters, we know this person is wanted, not needed. This again means they serve as a compliment to something that is already good or great.

If you are living life to the fullest, you should be able to continue this lifestyle with your lifelong mate, right? Of course, just remember that if the person you are with does not satisfy your number one want, you have already started on a path that is not headed in the right direction. Do not forget this person should be at least 70% - 75% similar to you, so those things that you enjoyed while being single and had you feeling as though you were living life to the fullest should be minimally compromised. For this particular reason, the prior chapters and stages in this book are crucial in the process of developing and knowing what steps to take when it comes to determining if this mate has potential to be the one. If you follow those steps, you will be in great shape when it comes to finding the partner that you can continue to flourish with day by day, month after month, and year after year until the end of time.

I do understand that once life takes its course, we develop obligations and responsibilities that alter our time. Even so, those are only excuses. When things in life are wanted, do what people do that usually get what they want do-PREPARE, PLAN, and then WORK YOUR PLAN. Just because you have kids does not mean you cannot go dancing or have a date night. Hire a baby sitter for the evening. If money is the problem, remember to prepare and plan. Try and save a few dollars a week to offset the upfront payment.

Plan a cruise and try to coordinate work vacations so you both can enjoy one another. If there is a want, there is a way.

Once you stop living life, it is just a matter of time before the relationship is truly over. I often hear people speak of how their mate sleeps in a different room and they live in the same home. They may never do anything together and rarely communicate. Some couples even mention no longer being intimate with each another. These behaviors and a host of other different things are immediate indicators that the roof has fallen in on their relationship. When these lines of communication start to break down, it is just a matter of time before the entire home caves in. Those situations are not only bad to be in, but they are also unhealthy for the mind, body, and soul to experience on a daily basis.

In closing, remember to seek the person you want, because this will allow you to experience the fullness of life on a stage that was made for two.

Activities

LST Task 11

List five things you like/liked to do while being single that you would like to continue doing if you were/are in a committed relationship.

Examples:

1. Go Dancing

2. Go Bowling

3. Shoot Pool

4. Go to plays or opera's

5. Sit at home and watch movies on a Friday night

Chapter Twelve

The Bottom Line
After it's all said and done...

We have looked hard and deep within ourselves to discover the one want that we must have. We have learned that this is the foundation we will stand on when searching for our lifelong mate. We also learned that we must first complete ourselves so that we do not need a mate to complete us; rather we want a mate that compliments us instead. Our journey took us to the depths of understanding the difference between a standard and a deal breaker. It showed us that if the characteristic or feature that we are questioning does not hold the same weight as our deal breakers it is considered a standard, which again is optional. Mars and Venus showed us the desires of a man and woman. It taught us that simplicity and focusing on these wants keeps the planets aligned.

We discussed that the coined phrase, "opposites attract" is not a valid statement when it comes to attracting that life-long mate. Our path led us to find that we do not have to take unrealistic leaps and bounds to connect with someone, but those small strides taken daily and consistently keeps us in the race for the long haul.

This conditioned us to understand that in order to receive a return; we must be willing to deposit and invest in our potential lifelong mate. Additionally, we concluded that this action is not performed after the decision has been made to become one. This commitment has to be made while going through the dating phase as we work towards developing a lifelong union until the very end. This gave us the ability to shake off the fact that we all have played the fool a time or two, making us better and not bitter because of it. The baggage that we held on for so long from playing the fool in our past has been cleansed. This baggage was affecting our actions in the present which was destroying our chance to be successful in the future.

Our journey has allowed us to understand the meaning of being in love vs. loving someone. As we found out, we must seek the concrete stage in our relationship because this level helps us withstand the tests of time. Our briefcases were left outside as we rushed home to meet our mate behind closed doors with plans to not only be that hard worker by day, but a fantasy at night. After satisfying one another physically and mentally with our intimate encounters, we found out that we must continue to live life and not fall into the hole of just living. Our relationship must continue to soar to higher limits day after day. We must continue to add wood to the fire that has made our flame for one another grow.

Onward we march to the end of our journey or should we say the start of building our religious and spiritual foundation also known as, "The Bottom Line". It does not matter how much effort you put into transferring these strategies and ideas you have acquired from this book into your everyday life if you do not commit totally to seeking a husband or a wife. If being a husband or a wife is not your purpose you are wasting your time. Be honest in your desire of being totally sold on wanting a husband or a wife before pursuing a lifelong mate. Use your "single time" to prepare yourself to be that compliment that you desire to be. Make sure you are putting the best potential lifelong mate forward at all times.

Finally, make sure you have a "guiding" foundation that will be able to help you appreciate the good times in a committed relationship. Also, allow this "guide" to support you through the tough times as well. A religious and spiritual foundation is recommended because it provides principles and guidelines that allow us to seek something or someone we trust and believe in as we grow as one with our partner. While on your journey with your lifelong mate if God serves as your higher source allow him to guide you and your mate as you grow into a union. If you believe in the Bible, let this tool be your instructional manual that will assist you in remaining aligned with his purpose. If your religious or spiritual perspectives lead you in a different direction that is okay.

I believe we all are entitled to select our individual preference when we speak of religion and spirituality.

If being on one accord with your mate is important discuss these views and perspectives in the beginning. As you search for your mate remember to stay true to your deal breakers. They will be important and will remain important until the end of time. I would like to wish you the best of luck on your search. I hope this book gives you hope, happiness, and the feeling that true love is right before your eyes. Just be patient, dedicated, and believe your lifelong mate is out there. We will live for love and for love we will live.

Activities
LST Task 12

If you have not done so, go back and complete all the tasks in this self-help manual in order to find your lifelong mate.

Bonus Chapter

The Relationship Window
Right Place, Right Time...

Have you ever wondered when your time will come to enjoy a healthy long lasting relationship? Maybe you keep telling yourself, "It's not my time" or how about the all-time favorite, "I'm waiting on God to send me my mate." Well let me open your mind to this possible perspective. As I pondered on the word, "time" it led me to entertain the word "timing".

Have you ever looked at meeting the right person as a situation that will definitely come within a certain window of opportunity? I believe a man and a woman have a certain time frame that opens and provides them with the best situation possible when it comes to finding one they are equivalent too or as many say, "equally yoked" with. This window opens multiple times throughout a person's life; however, it is up to the individual to make the best of it.

In this window frame of opportunity, you have a chance to grow and connect or the risk of possibly sacrificing valuable time with someone who really did not deserve it. The biggest players in this game are Mr. and Mrs. Maturity. As I think about the very essence of the word it is not a secret that research and studies have proven women mature more rapidly than men. This could play a huge role when it pertains to relationship maturity and a person's window frame of opportunity.

As we keep the maturity aspect in mind let's apply this to dating and seeking a lifelong mate. The level of maturity an individual elevates to is usually the main reason why a relationship succeeds or fails. This can cause those who experience numerous failures to avoid dating and seeking a relationship because we as human beings can only take so much before we begin to resent the very notion of desiring something that continues to bring us pain and heartache.

In my opinion most mature women desire something concrete and real as they enter their late 20's heading to their early 30's. By this time most mature women have attained numerous personal goals and aspirations and now want a family and the fairy tale lifestyle that many grew up hearing and dreaming about. However, most men during this age frame are not ready for those commitments and are not mature enough to truly understand their role as a man, husband, and father.

As I like to say, "We were sowing our royal oats" which could lead to divorce or an unhealthy relationship. So if a mature woman is fortunate enough to be found by a mature man who is equipped mentally, physically, emotionally, spiritually, and financially enough to handle the responsibilities that come along with those given titles during this time frame she is a lucky one.

As we take a look at the man. Most men start to reach a level of relationship maturity in their early 30's as they grow closer to being 40. By this time life has revealed his purpose and he embraces his opportunity not only to become one with life, yet to be a husband and a father. During this period, he will also desire a mature woman who aspires to be a wife and a mother. So if a mature man is fortunate enough to find a mature woman who is equipped mentally, physically, emotionally, spiritually, and financially to start a family with and live an abundant life he is also a lucky one. Unfortunately, by this time many women who are single may provide various reasons not to connect with this individual. Many have probably been married before and are now divorced. They may have been involved in an unhealthy relationship that they have not healed from. Some could possibly have children and do not desire more. Others may be at a place of independence where a lifelong relationship does not have the same zest on it as it did 5 or 6 years prior.

Then you may have those who have been through so much that being married is nowhere in the equation because of what they have had to overcome and it is not worth risking where they are now which is a place or peace and tranquility.

This really makes me believe as we mature, grow, and become of age we have windows of opportunity that open and close when it comes to finding a lifelong mate. This means that we have to really continue to work on making sure "self" is ready to receive our blessing when it presents itself. This means recycling the negative baggage that one may be still clinging on too. It means being open minded to different things as it pertains to dating and relationships and just simply helping God by doing your part as it pertains to doing his will and he will reward your efforts. So continue to work daily on being a better you and don't be surprised when your life long mates comes crawling through that window of opportunity that God will provide for you. There are millions of great people who desire what you desire and the awesome thing is you only need one to be mature enough to have a long lasting relationship.

About the Author

In addition to being an author, Dr. Marco Walder is an educator, life-skills instructor, mentor, speaker, and a poet. A native of Dallas, Texas, Marco earned a Bachelors of Science degree in Interdisciplinary Studies and a Masters of Education in Secondary Education from Alcorn State University. He also earned his Doctorate of Education in Sport and Athletic Management from Northcentral University. Dr. Marco Walder is an advocate for improving the academic performance and higher education graduation rates of student-athletes. During his undergraduate matriculation, he was a four-year letter winning football player.

Dr. Walder is a member of Phi Beta Sigma Fraternity, Incorporated and is an active member in his local community. Marco is a strong Christian and roots his message in a biblical foundation and he attends Concord Church under the leadership of Pastor Bryan

Carter. When he is not delivering motivational messages and speeches, he volunteers his efforts and energy to the Heads Up Foundation of Dallas which serves the youth leagues of Texas. Dr. Walder expresses real life and real hope for today's society. In addition to his latest book, "Beyond The Gridiron: A Look Into The Academic Preparation Of Urban High School Student Athletes", Dr. Walder has authored several previous titles and numerous articles.

A noted speaker, Dr. Walder has presented for Dallas Independent School District, the El Centro Community College TRIO program, the Brookhaven Community College Black History Month Expo, and at local schools including Maynard Jackson Middle School and Oliver Wendell Holmes. He has also ventured outside the state to various cities such as Lake Charles, LA and Gulfport, MS to share his positive and uplifting messages.

www.ingramcontent.com/pod-product-compliance
Lightning Source LLC
Chambersburg PA
CBHW071451070426
42452CB00039B/1137